Wilson's
Ushers' Guide

Compiled by
Mrs. Gertrude Reed & Miss S.B. Wilson

With Rules and Regulations
Suggested for Ushers' Boards and Religious Organizations

Wilson's

Ushers' Guide

WILSON'S USHERS' GUIDE
Copyright © 1998 by National Baptist Publishing Board
6717 Centennial Blvd.
Nashville, TN 37209-1049

ISBN 1-56742-005-2

All Scripture quotations, unless otherwise noted, are taken from the King James Version of the Bible or are the author's paraphrase of it.

Printed in the United States of America

✝

CONTENTS

✝

PREFACE

Feeling the need for a suggestive guide that will assist ushers and auxiliaries of similar nature in the providing of comfort, convenience, and the relieving of embarrassments upon members as well as strangers, visiting churches and religious organizations, I am impelled to impose my limited views with apologies for errors and omissions on an ever anxious, but a very discriminating populance. Because of this I am beginning my little booklet with a definition of the word "usher" and the word "board," and I am handling it or presenting it in a hyphenated word called "Usher-Board."

✝

THE LATE
MRS. GERTRUDE REED
Co-author of Revised Edition
of Wilson's Ushers' Guide

Mrs. Gertrude Reed was a dedicated, conscientious servant of the Lord. The impact and influence of her life has been felt by all those who knew her. It has been said that those who die in the Lord are blessed and that their works do follow them. Mrs. Reed's work continues to be a blessing to others.

As ushers, in churches around the country, faithfully serve as "doorkeepers in the house of the Lord," the influence of Mrs. Reed's work continues to be left.

✝

DEDICATED TO THE LATE
MISS SADIE B. WILSON
Nashville, Tennessee

Sadie Beulah Wilson was born in Williamson County, Tennessee to the late James and Sallie P. Wilson. She was the youngest of three daughters. In 1913, she graduated from Pearl High School, Nashville, Tennessee.

Miss Wilson became an employee of the National Baptist Publishing Board in 1914 and worked there for 52 years. She worked under three leaders of the National Baptist Publishing Board, Dr. R.H. Boyd, Dr. Henry Allen Boyd and Rev. T.B. Boyd, Jr. In her position as Secretary to Dr. Henry Allen Boyd, Miss Wilson traveled extensively, going to Europe, Canada, the Bahamas and practically every state in the United States.

She was a member of Mt. Olive Baptist Church and worked in almost every department of the church, giving her service where she felt she could save. She passed away in April of 1966 leaving a notable legacy of service.

FOREWORD

The contents of this guide have come forth from many years of experience as an usher, from training and from words and suggestions previously written by Miss Sadie B. Wilson found in the National Baptist Publishing Board's Ushers' Guide.

The rules suggested in this periodical are by no means exhaustive, but it is believed that they are basic in church ushering.

In reading this material, you will discover some repetition; however, this is done for the purpose of driving home, what seems to me to be, a pertinent thought that needs to be recognized and adhered to at all times.

The biblical references pointed out in this guide are believed to give scriptural background to the office of the usher. Although some of the duties of individuals who served as watchmen, porters, or doorkeepers before the coming of Christ into the world, are not identical with those of the present day usher, one must be motivated by the spirit of evangelism and exemplify a stewardship life.

"We are saved to help save others." We must help carry out Christ's program of salvation for the redemption of mankind. To do this helps us to become good stewards. For Christian stewardship is, "The acknowledgement of God's ownership, the acceptance of our trusteeship of life and possessions, and the administration of the same according to the will of God."

It is in the spirit of Christian stewardship that these suggestions are made to you. It is hoped that Christ will lead you from these humble thoughts on ushering to a

✝

broader and more meaningful life of service for Him. May the following ever be your watchword:

"For a day in thy courts is better than a thousand. I had rather be a doorkeeper in the house of my God, than to dwell in the tents of wickedness" (Psalm 84:10).

Your humble servant,
Gertrude Reed

✞

THE USHER

An usher is an officer of the church that he or she serves. An usher is one who introduces strangers, a doorkeeper, a forerunner, or one who walks before persons of rank.

DEFINITION OF AN USHER

There are many definitions of ushering. Here are a few basic meanings. Ushering means to show into a room, to introduce or escort into a room or seat.

Ambrose R. Clark, dean of New York Ushers, said, "Ushering is the art of making the members and visitors feel comfortable and of lending spiritual dignity to the whole church service."

Andrew Black said, "By promptness, courtesy, tact and unobtrusiveness, the usher helps the pastor and promotes worship."

EARLY HISTORY OF USHERING

Man has with knowledge and wisdom made many improvements in ushering, but everything we now enjoy, or may hereafter enjoy, was in the Creation.

Four thousand and four years before the coming of Christ, men were serving in the same capacity, similar to that of the present day usher.

Bible history teaches us in Numbers 1:48-53, that God directed Moses in the wilderness of Sinai, to organize what I would determine to be the great usher organization as watchmen over the Tabernacle of Testimony and over all vessels thereof, and over all things that belong to it and keep charge of the Tabernacle.

In Numbers 3:12, he claimed the Levites as his own. In 2 Samuel 18:24, 25, they are spoken of as watchmen. In 1 Chronicles 9:17, 21, 22, they are given the name of "Porters."

In 1 Chronicles 15:23, 24, they are called "Doorkeepers," this name lasted down across a number of years and centuries until today we find people rendering the same kind of service to the church, being referred to as ushers; but you will not find the word "usher" in the Bible.

In this, we see the usher has a wealth of biblical background and the church usher is claimed by our Lord as His own, for He says in His Word, "Therefore the Levites shall be mine." Since the usher is serving in the same capacity as the Levites, we must be chosen people.

The origin of the first usher's group in modern times was one thousand, one hundred and seven years after the birth of our Savior. Man felt he had discovered a new service for the church. It is true that these servants were given the name, church usher, at a later date; but all Bible students know that this service had its beginning in the Creation.

The first usher's group in modern times was organized by Mr. Ambrose R. Clark of New York, in 1897, in an endeavor to improve church ushering. His purpose and procedure or organization became the foundation of modern organized church ushering.

✟

CHURCH USHERS' ASSOCIATION

On January 10, 1914, ushers from twenty-three New York churches met and organized the first Church Ushers' Association. This was to promote and develop a kindred Christian fellowship through ushering in the various churches represented in the association. Since then this idea has spread throughout the United States. Today, it has become an independent organization.

This organization was the outgrowth of informal discussion which had been going on since March, 1910, with the thought that the exchange of ideas on church ushering and ushering at public meetings with a religious purpose, was an important factor in the religious metropolis.

THE USHER'S BOOK

The first Usher's Guide for church ushers was published and produced by the Church Ushers' Association of New York in 1910. In 1924, Fleming H. Revel Co., published a book entitled "Church Usher's Manual," by Willis O. Garrett, pastor of First Presbyterian Church, Miami, Florida.

This standard work still has wide acceptance, but since that time many more books have been published by various denominations. Today, more than ever, there is an increasing interest in this important art.

CHURCH USHER'S PRAYER

"In the name of the Father and the Son and the Holy Ghost, Bless O Lord, this Thy servant, as Thou didst bless the son of Levi who ministered in Thy Holy Temple, and

☦

grant me devoutly to minister in Thy house and Thy name be hallowed; Thy Kingdom come, and thy will be done; through Jesus Christ, Thy Son, our Lord, Amen."

THE USHER'S PSALM

The Lord is my light. He is the joy of my salvation, of whom then shall I be afraid.

I am a doorkeeper in the house of the Lord. Yea though I meet with unpleasant conditions, I must keep smiling, for I must enter into His presence with thanksgiving and into His courts with praise.

Yea, though I walk through the shadow of kindness, I must smile, for the beauty of the Lord is upon me; my countenance is filled with light, the light of love, patience and endurance. I shall strive to give joy to the sorrowful, hope to the lost, sunshine to the darkness, and I shall remain a doorkeeper in the house of the Lord, as long as I live.

USHER'S PLATFORM

Preamble: "I had rather be a doorkeeper in the house of my God, than to dwell in the tents of wickedness" (Psalm 84:10).

Aim: To serve the Lord Jesus, through the service they render to humanity.

Motto: Ready to serve. "Knowing that of the Lord ye shall receive the reward of the inheritance: for ye serve the Lord Christ" (Colossians 3:24).

✝

Watch-word: Study. "Study to show thyself approved unto God, a workman that needeth not to be ashamed, rightly dividing the word of truth" (2 Timothy 2:15).

USHER'S PLEDGE

I pledge by the help of God to do my best to serve my church with a pure heart, clean hands, and a breath that will not be offensive to those I welcome into the house of the Lord.

I further pledge to abide by the rules and regulations of the board and my superior officers; to attend my meetings and serve when called upon, unless I can give a reasonable excuse; and to keep my financial obligations of the board as near as possible.

USHER'S UNIFORMS

Ladies uniforms must be made of the same material, color, and pattern.

If the ladies uniforms are white, pink slips should not be worn unless they are a part of the uniform. Black slips should be worn under black uniforms.

Shoes should be of the same color and the heels must not be out. Hose should be of the same shade.

No lady should attempt to usher without a good foundation garment. Ladies must not wear fancy combs or flowers in their hair, or large fancy earrings, or chest ornaments unless it is voted part of their uniform.

All men ushers should wear suits of the same shade and the coat should be double-breasted and buttoned at all times while in service.

✞

Men must be shaved and hair must be in order to serve. Men usher's shoes must be shined when they report for duty. Men's shirts must be of the same color. The color and style of ties, as well as all other parts of the uniform, must be voted on by the board.

As ushers, we should always keep in mind this motto: "If every usher was just like me, what would this usher's group be?"

The usher must keep in mind he/she is not a department store model. His or her appearance should be in keeping with the high position they are filling. Always be neat in appearance.

SIX QUALIFICATIONS FOR AN USHER

I. CHRISTIANITY

To be a good church usher, you must be a Christian. A Christian is one who professes Jesus Christ as Savior, and accepts Him as his Lord.

Christianity is the precept and doctrine taught by Christ.

The usher holds an exalted position in the church, yet some of the Christian ushers are not filling their positions as God would have them.

When persons are converted, they are changed from what they once were. They are cleansed from sin. You should realize that when you leave the Devil's army, he will do all he can to gain you back. Sometimes he will use your best friend as a forerunner.

✝

Some Christians think they have a hard road to travel, yet our Savior tells us, "For my yoke is easy, and my burden is light" (Matthew 11:30).

Some ushers never go to prayer meeting nor take the Lord's Supper. God's Word tells us, "Not forsaking the assembling of ourselves together" (Hebrews 10:25). Christ said that as often as we partake of the Lord's Supper, this we do in remembrance of Him, of His suffering and death for us (1 Corinthians 11:24-26).

Ushers are considered servants because of the office they hold in the church. There is one class of ushers who display their Christianity on Sunday morning only. God is not pleased with this. He wants us to be willing to serve Him at all times.

Ushers should exercise much care in receiving the guests in the church. The usher should greet the guest with a sober mind, a pleasant smile and a kind word.

Unless the ushers possess that true doctrine taught by our Savior and are filled with that true love of God in their hearts, they are out of harmony with what Christianity stands for.

II. COURTESY

The one outstanding trait of an usher is to be courteous. That is the watch word at all services. If we fail to be courteous to all guests, especially the poor, lame and the blind, we have failed Christ just that much.

No person should attempt to serve as a church usher, who does not have the urgent need of true fellowship, a loving personality and a pleasant smile. Of course, one is not expected to smile at all times, but never frown when others display their temper. The best way to handle one who does display his temper, is to be polite, smile, and if appropriate, say, "I'm sorry."

Some people leave home out of sorts and the first person they meet at the entrance of the church is the usher. But, if you keep in mind that 5th chapter of Matthew and the 16th verse, which reads: "Let your light so shine before men, that they may see your good works, and glorify your Father which is in heaven," you will be able to meet any situation that arises.

When you fully realize your position and responsibility to the church, it will not be a burden to smile and be polite to the most discourteous person. The word "courteous'" will become your second nature and frown will be unknown.

Ushers have a great opportunity to be of great service to their church and to their Savior.

We will do well to remember the words of Abraham Lincoln who said, "With malice toward none and charity for all, let us set forth a new nation unto God, that the government of the people, for the people and by the people, shall not perish from the earth." As the bending sky surpasses the clouds which drift across it, so stands the lasting laws of love, justice, mercy, truth and courtesy." The usher may also say as the apostle Paul, "Do all things without murmuring and disputings: That ye may be blameless and harmless" (Philippians 2:14-15a).

III. ALERTNESS OF AN USHER

The word "alert" means to always be on the watch – quick to act. To be a good usher, you must be on the look-

✝

out for the crippled, the sick, fires, or any other emergency that may arise.

You should be alert to keep down evil or confusion you may sense arising in your board. Be on the alert for any necessary or urgent calls, or anything the pastor may need you for. It takes all these things to be an alert usher.

IV. PROMPTNESS

One of the six qualifications of a good church usher is promptness. To be prompt means to be quick to act as the occasion demands. An usher that is prompt is an asset to his or her leader. He does not have to wonder if the usher will be on time or if he will have enough ushers to fill the stations.

Promptness in an usher can manifest itself intelligently in a crucial moment. Should a fire break out in a crowded place, this usher can see to is that he/she or someone else tries to extinguish it with as little confusion as possible, and tries to keep the audience calm to prevent their becoming panicky.

Promptness in an usher is essential.

V. COURAGEOUSNESS

Another qualification of a good usher is 'courageousness.' A courageous usher is one who can face life with a smile when things are not so pleasant; can meet his obligations, sorrows, and joys, half-way.

Courageous is the usher who strives to lift his fellowman to a better understanding toward "peace on earth and good will toward mankind."

☥

Ushers should work courageously and never doubt himself of herself, and be always ready to give a helping hand where needed.

We as ushers, to win, must fortify our lives with courage for the conflicts that arise. The courageous usher will never give up, no matter how badly wounded. He/she will carry on just the same.

Ushers should never become so discouraged that they will have their task undone because of being criticized or ridiculed.

For one to be a courageous usher, one must have faith in God, for only faith in God and in His way of life, can give us the courage we need to face the test of life.

VI. DISCIPLINE

The one great factor of success in any usher group is the discipline with which it is controlled. Our guidance must come from within, motivated by our love for God and for our work.

The most successful group of ushers are those that adhere to God's guidance in accepting the position as doorkeeper in the house of God. This should cause one to think of his actions in his daily life and realize that self-discipline should cause one to know that taking part in worldly activities would lessen the respect others have for you in the position you hold in your church.

The better your training and the greater the discipline, the better appearance your group makes and the smoother your work will be.

SOME THINGS TO REMEMBER

An usher must remember to be an individual, but not personal. Do not chat together when on duty; be punctual; be dignified; remain at your post and do not wander around the church.

When you are not ushering, you should participate in the service.

Do not show any mark of displeasure when people do not follow you to the seat you have for them, but leave you strolling down the aisle alone. Just smile as if it is alright.

Be on time and attend your usher meetings, especially your instruction meetings. Remember, your work is important. You serve the Lord, Jesus Christ, and you are a part of the worshipping congregation.

Do your work quietly, friendly and courteously. Follow the wishes of the pastor and the governing board. Notify your head usher promptly if you cannot serve on your Sunday. By all means, try to improve yourself. Do not chew gum while on duty.

I. THE CHURCH USHER SHOULD LOVE

The essence of God is love. "Let all we do, be done in love." Therefore, an usher should love his fellowman. There is one quality an usher must have before he is chosen, that is one of the basic requirements, "Love for his fellowman."

Lacking this quality, he will never make a good usher. If he is indifferent toward his fellowman, he is not ready to represent God's church.

✞

II. THE USHER REPRESENTS THE CHURCH

The usher stands for, and is part of the church. The usher is the first person the worshipper comes into contact with, and he must show individual interest to each one.

The usher's personality, words and acts will largely set the tempo of the church service and may determine whether or not people come back again. It is an honor to be a church usher.

OFFICERS OF THE USHER BOARD

An usher group should consist of a full set of officers, viz: president, a chairman or chief usher, a vice-chairman or vice-president, a recording secretary, treasurer, and a chairman of the sick committee.

The chairman or president should preside at all meetings, but if the chairman or president is absent, then the vice-chairman or vice-president should be called; if neither the chairman, president, vice-chairman, nor vice-president is present, the chief usher, or either one of the secretaries present, should call the meeting to order and the group may select a temporary or pro tem presiding officer.

The recording secretary should record all minutes in a well bound book, reading the minutes at the next meeting or whenever called upon to do so, recording all motions and acts of the usher group.

The corresponding secretary should take care of all correspondence; have the names and addresses of all members of the board and notify them of each regular or special meetings, and should send out notices to the other members when one of their members is sick.

The treasurer should receive all monies from the group and report the same to the church, according to the policies of the church.

All officers should serve for one year, or until their successors have been elected and qualified. A failure to elect at any annual meeting does not invalidate the term or office for the incumbent, but they should hold office until their successors are chosen or appointed, whichever is the practice of the church.

DUTIES OF THE PRESIDENT

The president of an usher group holds a very responsible position in the church. The main principles of leadership are few in number and simple in understanding.

The principles are the coordination of these four qualities: to organize, to deputize, to visualize and to supervise.

A good president of an usher group must be qualified to see in every detail and as a complete whole that the task in the church is well-done. He must be able to organize the group so that its task can be done most efficiently and with the least amount of friction or wasted energy.

He or she must be able to choose the right person to carry out the specialized duties of the organization, and to delegate authority to them. He must be able to supervise, inspire and stimulate these helpers so there will be no working at cross purposes or duplication of effort at the cost of the groups' efficiency.

Some of the responsibilities the president of the church usher group shoulders:

The ushers are hosts and hostesses of the church. The president is responsible to the church for the conduct of the group while on duty.

As the usher group is a financial unit of the church, the president should see to it that the group lives up to its financial obligations as well.

The responsibility of the president is to the members of the group. It is here he can display the finest form of leadership. He must supervise the personnel of the group in such a way as not to permit the overlapping of duties and authorities.

Since this is one of the most harmful conditions in any organization, the exact definition of duties and power merits the most serious consideration on the part of the president. He must be tactful in keeping the group working in peace and harmony at all times.

The president is responsible to church-goers for the way they are treated by the ushers from the time they enter the church until they leave.

The president should be at church in time to contact the pastor and to get the orders of the day before time for the ushers to assemble. When the ushers are assembled, prayer should be offered, thanking God for them being permitted to come together and asking His divine guidance through the day.

The president should let the orders of the day be known and make the duty appointments. The president should know the church's program and must be well versed in the art of ushering.

✝

One cannot tell anyone how to do something when one does not know himself. For this reason, a study course is suggested for all ushers, at least once a year.

QUALIFICATIONS FOR USHER LEADERSHIP

To be a good instructor of a church usher group, one must be a good leader. What is a leader?

Webster says, "a leader is one who leads, a commander, a guide, a conductor, the chief of a party." But be reminded of one thing, that everyone who is elected the head of an organization, or group of people, is not always a leader.

The one who actually leads is the one with the most influence. So, first, to be the leader, you must try to be the most influential member of your group.

Second, you must develop your group's confidence. You can go a long way in doing this by knowing what to do and when to do it.

Prepare yourself for the position before you aspire for it. Then, you will know what to say and when to say it.

If someone in your group seeks answer to legitimate questions and you cannot answer them, it becomes evident you do not know what you should do, and the one that gives the answer to the questions, is the one they look to as their guide or leader.

If you have prepared yourself, then you will know all the necessary answers, and they will have confidence in you. If once you have their trust, it becomes an easy task to lead them. But, above all things, do your utmost to never betray that trust. Do all you can to stimulate their interest in

✝

their work; encourage them even though they are not so good and they will become better in their service.

Handle your group as individuals, for there are not two people alike. Show an individual interest in each of them; make them feel that you are doing all you can to help them, and they will do a much better job.

When speaking to your group or an individual, speak distinctly and at a moderate rate of speed, use simple and direct English and all will understand what you are saying.

RELIGIOUS AND MORAL CHARACTERISTICS OF AN USHER LEADER

Consecration is a prime requisite of Christian leadership. You must be a consecrated Christian.

Consecration is making one's life count for Christ. It is one of the great essentials in Christian work. There should be no doubt as to the sincerity of one's religious profession and spiritual qualifications for Christian usher leadership.

A consecrated leader is one who abides in Christ. As the saying goes, "religious truths can be taught, but the religious spirit must be caught."

It is required that a leader have the Spirit of Christ, which is the Spirit of unselfishness.

I remember reading of a student retreat where each member was asked to tell why he had come. Every member had come just to get something except one. That person said, "I came to get all I could, but I have also come to give all the help I can from my few years of experience."

✝

GUIDE TO LEADERSHIP

1. Pray ever to God that He will lead you, that you may lead others.
2. Put all you have into what you are doing. Do the task at hand as though your entire future depended on it.
3. It is said, growth comes through responsibility. Then, seek it! Do not try to avoid it. You must take life as an essential adventure.
4. Prepare today for what you hope to do tomorrow, and always give more than you receive and you are on the road to achievement.
5. Have as your motto: "Boldness with common sense and tact."
6. Develop a good "follow through." As we all know, persistence to every detail is a vital element to success.
7. Let your decision be clear-cut after you have all the facts.
8. Don't worry about who will get the credit.
9. Always be a good listener.
10. You must be very specific.
11. Put yourself in the other fellow's shoes before you give orders, or make quick decisions.
12. Be extremely quick to pay compliments where deserved. If you must criticize, do it in private.
13. Above all, never build yourself at the other persons expense. Their friendship and cooperation is immensely more important than any monetary gain.
14. Do your best to cultivate a friendly feeling toward those you don't like. Do all you can to appreciate

✟

their good qualities. Always remember, "there is some good in all of us; and some bad in the best of us."

15. Live one day at a time.
16. At the end of each day, thank God for the success of that day.

USHER'S PRAYERFUL SPIRIT

The usher should have a reverent, prayerful spirit. By praying more, you will not work less, but will accomplish more. You don't have to pray out loud, you can whisper a prayer as you work. Prayer is not all talking, but it is listening to God as well.

It was Samuel who said, "Speak Lord, for Thy servant heareth."

Prayer drives away discouragement and builds up faith and zeal. It strengthens you and makes you more aware of your task.

As ushers, keep this in mind: Blessed is the usher who grasps the meaning of Christ's Words, "He that is greatest among you, shall be your servant."

WHY WE NEED LEADERSHIP

Leadership is human management, and human management is a difficult job. We need leaders because an overwhelming majority of the human race are prone followers and just drift with the crowd.

The need for leadership is immeasurably great and the field of church ushering is no different. The modern church usher is a psychologically different usher from his predecessor. Church ushering today, is a fascinating systematized art that is acquired only after painstaking study of the work.

Close study of, and genuine interest in every member of your group will enable you to take your place as a great leader.

A leader possessing high ideals will seek to have the spirit of love ruling in his heart.

A few things a leader of an usher group should avoid:

Hate; a proud look; a lying tongue; a heart that deviseth wickedness; a false witness that speaketh lies; and he that soweth these things strikes discord among the brethren.

It is encouraging to know a leader is not static, but grows under heavy responsibility. It may take days, even months, but there will come a degree of improvement.

Leaders are not all born, they can be made unless they possess some definite quality that would disqualify them. By faithful study and prayerful work, they can learn. While helping others to grow, they are strengthening themselves by using the gift God has given them.

Jesus was an ideal leader. He willingly spent 30 years training for three years' work. How many of us would do that? We would want to do just the opposite, train three years for 30 years' work.

A leader of an usher auxiliary must be willing to work. If a leader of ushers expects to follow Jesus, he must not be afraid to work. Jesus was not afraid of manual labor. As a lad, he toiled in Joseph's carpenter shop and went out to do a greater work, to proclaim He was the "Bread of Life, and the Light of the World."

✢

Leading is hard, but the joy you get out of it makes it easy. Christ accomplished the purpose for which He came into the world. Let all who are leaders follow Him.

THE TECHNIQUES OF USHERING

The usher's techniques differ from the chores of the custodian, but the usher must have the know-how if he is going to do his job in a commendable way.

If an usher is ill-at-ease and not familiar with the procedure of his job, it is almost certain his performance will be below standard.

But, if the usher has mastered the techniques of his job, he can accomplish his purpose with the same ease as a good automobile driver displays in operating his car.

When greeting guests, smile, walk backward a few steps and if they seem willing to follow you, turn and walk forward, keeping just a few steps ahead of them, keeping in whispering distance, for if you go galloping down the aisle too far ahead of your guests, they may be unable to warn you if they decide to sit in a vacant seat near the rear of the church. This will leave you to proceed alone down the aisle and you will be embarrassed when you turn to seat your guests and find you are alone.

If you keep a few steps ahead of them, and walk moderately slow, you will be quite accessible, if they decide not to follow you to the front. Each time you seat a person, try to spot all the vacant seats in your section and know just how many you can seat. Also note, whether seats are single or double, for larger or smaller persons, and let the usher at the entrance of the aisle know by a

✝

sign so he/she will not send too many down and you will not have space for them.

As near as possible, seat the early arrivals to the front, leaving the rear seats for the late ones; but, as you know, there are some people who definitely prefer sitting in the rear of the church, this cannot be changed.

Regular church attenders, over a period of years seem to want the same seat. If you are alert, it will not be difficult to recognize those people.

When the old timers arrive, take them to the pew where they are accustomed to being seated, if it is not filled. They will be flattered to know you remember where they like to sit.

Do not get in the habit of pointing people to seats rather than ushering them. That is a mark of poor ushering. If people do not cooperate with you as you try to find them an acceptable seat, let them go by themselves; but be sure you never point to a seat or that your are never guilty of ignoring them.

Try to seat people with small children near the rear, if you can. So often they are getting up, climbing over people, going in and out with the children, and it is very disturbing to those who are trying to get something out of the service. It is also disturbing to the minister.

Anticipate the time of the offering. Have the offering plates in the hands of the ushers who are to serve and be sure they are ready and on time when called for. See to it that each usher knows his station. It looks very bad to see a group of ushers arrive at the front not knowing how to organize themselves to receive the offering.

✝

Every time the ushers are called to the front by the pastor, whether it be for the offering, or some duty during the service, they should walk in step. It makes a better appearance.

Be at ease in all your work. You cannot render efficient service if you are ill-at-ease in your talk. Learn to smile pleasantly and to walk with a sense of self-assuredness. That makes people realize you feel competent in your job.

Never seat people during prayer, Scripture reading, special numbers, or when the official notices are being read. Do not take people up front after the minister takes his text. As a rule, there are seats in the rear and in the side aisles.

In case of emergency, take full charge and handle it with a minimum of disturbance. If someone faints or becomes ill during the service, take that person out and call the doctor or first aid nurse. Do not cause any more confusion than necessary.

Ushers who learn to handle emergencies efficiently, help to save the spiritual part of the service when otherwise it could be ruined.

If children leave their seats during the service, it is best to hold them in the rear when they return. It may not disturb the minister, but the minds of people will be distracted from the sermon, especially if the youngsters are permitted to walk back and forth in the aisles and to climb in and out of pews.

Some youngsters, who are held back at the rear after they have walked out, soon catch on to the idea of why they are being kept in the rear and are cured of the habit.

✝

Ushers should be on duty at the Sunday church school hour, as well as morning and night services. All church services should be carried on in a spirit of worship. The usher who does not contribute to the spirit, makes himself a problem.

It is not the ushers' place to pass back and forth across the church; or go in and out of doors; or sit back and laugh or talk or hold a conversation, while service is in progress. They should sit in a very quiet way and in a spirit of prayer and reverence.

The usher cannot be told his every move. Except for knowing a few general techniques, the usher's worth depends largely on his ability to sense the fitness of things.

When off duty, ushers seated in the rear should be as quiet as possible. Noisy ushers indicate poor training, no respect for leadership or just plain ignorance.

THREE PROBLEM TYPES OF PEOPLE

The end-seater, who makes people climb over him, may be a claustrophobic (afraid to be closed in) and is not selfish in desire.

The middle-seater, who must sit away from the end, may be an agoraphobic (afraid of open spaces).

The same-seater, the person who has used the same pew for twenty years, would feel strange in another section.

The immovable may have reasons not to change places.

Each with his own desire, reasonable or seemingly unreasonable, has a right to his opinions. As the usher becomes aware of these spoken or unspoken requests, he should grant them when possible.

✝

PLACING USHERS IN THE AISLES

All ushers should be placed in the aisles and at the door at the beginning of the prayer service. If the ushers are placed in the aisle before the choir marches in, they should be pulled to the back of the church, facing the aisles that are being used for the processional.

When the last choir member passes, the usher should come to the center of the aisle and face the front. When the last choir member is four pews from the front of the sanctuary, all ushers are to follow, will move to their respective stations and get in service position.

During this time, the doorkeeper holds the guests in the vestibule until the choir has reached the choir stand and is facing the front.

All doorkeepers are to be relieved every 30 minutes. The aisle usher is to be relieved every 15 to 30 minutes.

In some churches, the ushers stand with their backs to the pulpit when in service position. But, others feel it is showing disrespect to the pulpit to stand with your back to it and find they can see the guests approaching when standing sideways in the middle of the aisle.

The latest service position is for the lady ushers to stand with their right hand cupped in their left hand, crossing the right. During the Scripture reading, special numbers, reading of official notices, and in some churches, during an anthem, the aisle ushers face the front, still in service position.

Anytime the ushers are facing the front, the doorkeepers hold the guests in the rear, for there will be no seating until the usher turns back sideways in a service position.

The men at the door, in service position, stand with their right hand crossing the left; and for prayer, their left hand crossing the right.

All ushers, when walking, drop their hands to their sides, but do not swing them any more than necessary.

USHERS IN THE BALCONY

Ushers should be placed in the balcony the same time they are placed on the main floor. The doors should be guarded at all times during the service.

When the ushers on the main floor are called to the front for prayer, the ushers in the balcony go down to the railing. After prayer, all ushering is done from this point and as the front pews are filled, they move up.

The offering in the balcony is received in the same manner and when completed, is turned over to the captain, who in turn, takes it to the proper place.

CHANGING STATIONS

All stations are changed at the same time. If there are two or more ushers in the aisle, those who are to change positions, come to the head of the aisle. The one who is to change with the front usher, starts off first, and when they get as far from the first usher as the one who is to change, the second usher is the same distance. Then he/she starts from the rear and each will reach his/her stations at the same time. When the usher gets within two or three steps of the usher to be changed, that usher takes one step forward. When the usher reaches them, they should stand behind them facing the front, until they turn right-about face and start off the station. The one taking their place turns, facing the center section and gets in service position, ready to receive the next guest.

Be sure to look for vacant seats. When the minister takes his text, all aisle ushers turn and go to the rear of the aisle. The one that the head usher or captain signals to stay at that point, will do all ushering from there.

In changing stations, always go down behind the usher who is already on the station. But, in coming off the station, always come back in front of the usher taking the station.

At all other times, when it becomes necessary to go up or down the aisle, always go in the back of the usher on the aisle.

CROSSING THE PULPIT

It is the duty of the usher not to let anyone cross in front of the pulpit at anytime during a service, and especially when someone is speaking or the minister is preaching.

The pulpit is a sacred place and it shows lack of respect when this rule is not observed.

No layman or laywoman should stand behind the pulpit when speaking or making announcements unless given permission from the minister. If they do not have a speaker's stand, then you just stand beside the pulpit.

USE OF BOOK RACKS

In churches that have book racks on the back of the pews, it is the duty of the president, or whoever is in charge, to arrive early enough to see that hymn books, envelopes and pencils are placed in the racks before service begins.

Bulletins should either be passed out at the door or by the aisle usher. By the aisle usher giving them out, it sometimes encourages the guests to follow them to the seat they have for them. But, in large churches where crowds are heavy, it is better to have them given out at the door.

NURSERY

Churches having a nursery, should make it known from the pulpit or through the bulletin at various times, and should be followed up by the ushers.

People will be proud to know you have a well attended nursery where they can leave the little ones while they enjoy the service.

SEATING THE GUESTS

If you are going to seat your guests on the right side of the aisle, use your right hand. If they are to be seated on the left side, use your left hand to direct them to their seat. Never cross yourself.

If you observe your guests very closely, you will know which section they would like to sit in, for they usually cast their eyes in that direction.

THREE-AISLE USHERING TECHNIQUES SHUTTLE FIXED-POST AND MIXED SHUTTLE AND POST

There are three methods or techniques of seating people. In the first one, the usher brings the worshipper up the aisle to the seat; and in the other, (fixed-post) the usher is already up the aisle, indicating where the worshipper is to be seated.

These two can be worked together. If so, they are called the mixed (Shuttle and Post) method.

Escorting the guest up the aisle is called the "Shuttle" method. The other is called the "fixed-post method." Each method has advantages and disadvantages.

SHUTTLE – IF THE AISLES ARE SHORT

The Shuttle Method is more satisfactory where the aisles are very short. It gives the worshipper more individual attention. It minimizes the chance of the worshipper trying to sit down in a location which is not suitable.

This technique should be used in churches which have the old method of rented or reserved seats.

The objections to this method being used alone are: (1) It requires much walking back and forth by the usher; (2) It requires every usher to be acquainted with all vacancies on the entire aisle – something that may be difficult if the aisles are long; (3) It generally requires more ushers than the "Fixed-Post" or the "Post and Shuttle" method, if the aisles are long.

FIXED POST – FOR LARGER CONGREGATIONS

The Fixed-Post method stations the ushers at fixed locations on the aisle, and passes the people on the next ushers. This method minimizes the number of vacancies any one usher has to be acquainted with. It makes certain

✠

no other usher has filled a vacancy while the first usher was going back to get the next worshipper.

When the two techniques are used together as Mixed Post and Shuttle, the usher who is bringing the worshipper up the aisle will get the seat location from the usher at the selected pew. He will bring the worshipper within a short distance of the usher at the pew, who in turn will seat them.

To seat guests, an usher should never put his hand on the back of the seat where the worshipper is to be seated. It seems too strong an invitation. Only give them an indication of the seat where they are to be seated with a polite gesture of the hand.

People who once have been seated, should not be moved when other vacancies arise unless the place where they are seems a little too crowded. Otherwise, they should be given new arrivals.

✝

**Position of both Ladies and Men when walking.
Both hands down to the sides.**

Receiving the Guest in the Church.

**Position of the Male Usher at the time of prayer.
Left hand over the right.**

Ladies' Service Position.
Standing sideways in aisle with right hand cupped
in the left, just a little below the waist.

Men's Service Position.
Standing right hand crossed over the left.

Prayer Position.
Face the altar with bowed heads and
left hand over the right.

LIFTING THE OFFERING

When lifting the offering, you should never start from the very back pew. The head usher or captain should know how many pews are in the center section. If you place six ushers in the two center aisles, three to each side of the center section, and three to each side of the side section, the ushers that are to lift the offering from the rear pews, should start several pews from the rear and work back. Then the people will know you are coming and can have their offering ready.

Ushers that march down together, should be near the same height if possible. Plates are picked up in the back of the church. The usher holds them in front with both hands; then march down the aisle by twos until the first pew is reached. The one on the right starts the plate down the second row, always using the right hand to pass the plate with; and also to receive it.

Always watch the plate coming to you. If the one coming to you gets to you before the other usher receives the plate you sent, just hold it until they are ready to start the plate back to you. This way you will finish together.

The usher assisting the choir, when finished, will come down and stand on the first step leading from the pulpit and remain there until the ushers on the floor have finished. Then they will all march back at the same time.

In churches where the ushers march to the front for prayer before lifting the offering, the head usher or captain, at the end of the prayer, will hand the plates to the ushers and at a sign they will go to their stations and start lifting the offering. When finished, all form a line by twos in the rear and march to the front with the plates where they will be turned over to the pastor or someone in charge for the prayer of thanksgiving. The ushers then return to the rear of the church.

INSTRUCTOR

All ushers should have a competent instructor and should hold an instruction meeting once every month, and every member should be required to participate in it.

Every member should be required to make at least one meeting every two months, and without a good excuse should not be qualified to work until they have made an instruction meeting.

No new usher should be eligible to work until he/she has attended the instruction meeting and have been properly instructed as to the rules and regulations of the group; properly uniformed; and have become familiar with the signal code and all the working procedures of the group.

Nothing new should be started on the floor on Sundays without first being talked over with the instructor and rehearsed in the instruction meeting.

SIGNAL CODE

All ushers should have a signal code. But, the ushers in cooperation with the pastor, should work out a system of signals. These signals should be more by the hand, rather than by the arm.

Where there is an association of ushers, they should have the same system of signals, so when working together, they will all understand the signals when given by any member of the association.

OBEDIENT USHERS

Ushers who want to increase their learning, will attend their instruction meetings.

We read in Proverbs 1:5-7, "A wise man will hear and will increase learning…but fools despise wisdom and instruction." So, be careful, do not let this apply to you.

THE CHURCH USHERS AND THEIR SERVICE

I use the word 'service' because the word, job, as Webster defines it, is to "let out for hire, any scheme for making money."

Since church ushering is a sacrificial service, I feel the most appropriate word to be used in describing the usher and his work, is "service."

The purpose of the church usher is to promote the divine worship of the church. To render service of any kind, effectively, there must be some preparation made.

Therefore, the first thing the usher must do is establish a setting appropriate for worship. As the people gather and are seated in the church, an atmosphere of worship can be created by seeing that they assemble in an orderly manner, and that a spirit of quietness and reverence prevails in, and around the church building.

For it is written, "But the Lord is in his holy temple: let all the earth keep silence before him" (Habakkuk 2:20).

Maintaining order and decency is one of the objectives of the church usher. There are a few directions God has given for examples of public worship.

✝

"Let all things be done decently and in order" (1 Corinthians 14:40).

Silently, they express the welcome to the church; they are interested in the comforts and needs of the worshippers; their desire is to make everyone comfortable.

The presence of God in church and the use of His Holy Word, require reverence, in the way service is conducted; and the manner in which the ushers behave themselves.

Acting as servants of the church over which the Lord has made the minister the host, the ushers have the privileges of expressing the invitation, "Come unto me" (Matthew 11:28). For they are servants in the house of the Lord.

For those who visit a church that uses the service of ushers, it means the elimination of things that would make it difficult to enter a new place; to face unusual situations; and to be among strangers.

To the members of the church, it means their presence is valuable.

The service of the usher is to be commended, for they serve as good soldiers no matter what the test may be. They stand, they accept the criticism of others and act with poise and dignity in difficult situations.

Anyone who knows the work of the church will agree that the services of the ushers are important. Their service influences, not only the work of the minister, the choir, the pianist, but the entire congregation.

Ushers should thank God for being permitted to render service in His church.

✝

OTHER DUTIES OF AN USHER

There are many duties required of the ushers. Their duties do not end with caring for the Sunday services, they are to be present at all weekly services, such as prayer services, programs, revivals and conventions.

KNOW YOUR CHURCH BUILDING

It is necessary for the ushers to know every part of their church building. Oft times visitors come and would like to see them through the building and it is the duty of the ushers to take them.

If you do not know the building yourself, you won't know where to start.

Sometimes they will want to know the location of the rest rooms, drinking fountains, dining room, offices, nursery and various parts of the building.

An usher should be well versed in these things. If you do not know all of these things and others I have not mentioned, you will not be considered an alert usher.

SEATING THE YOUNG PEOPLE

The best policy is to place young people near some interested and responsible adult. By no means put a gang of wiggling adolescents together on a back pew. They create too much disturbance. Scatter the ones most likely to disturb throughout the congregation.

In case the young people will not allow the usher to seat them, when the usher is off duty, try to win their friendship and solicit their cooperation.

✞

FUNERALS

Ushers should be present in uniform at all funerals. Oft times the funeral director has his own men trained to take care of the ushering, but you are there to assist in case the funeral director should need help.

Whenever death occurs in your usher group, all the members of your group should attend at visiting hours in their uniforms. Two members should be placed at the casket during the visitation hours to assist the family and friends in viewing the remains.

One usher should be placed at the register to see that each person, aside from the family, is registered.

Whenever an usher passes in a church, having more than one group, all groups should turn out in uniform at the funeral and sit in a body, expressing sympathy to the associate usher group, as they are "all members of One body."

THE USHER, A SOUL WINNER IN EVANGELISTIC SERVICE

Doing the work of soul winning in an evangelistic service should be one of the most important objectives of an usher. By faithful service their aim is to win souls for Christ.

But, to be a soul winner, you must have Bible knowledge. It is imperative that you, at least know enough of the Bible to make use of it.

It is the Word of Power – the Word of Conviction – and the Word of Cleansing.

✝

Today, the work of Evangelism is largely done by attracting sinners, backsliders and the weak Christian to a desire of wanting to attend church where they can hear God speak through His minister.

It is the ushers' aim to attract men, women, boys and girls to the realism of needing the Saviour. Once they have been able to interest people to attend church, they should put forth every effort to encourage their continued attendance. Eventually, they will become members.

THE CHURCH USHER AS GOD'S STEWARD

The word "Steward" or "Stewardship" occurs in the Bible some twenty-two times. Its basic meaning is, "One to whom something has been entrusted for supervision and management on behalf of another."

Christian stewardship rests upon the character of God as revealed in the Bible and specifically in Jesus Christ, His Incarnate Son.

Few ushers realize they are Christ's stewards and that through their service God will bless them richly.

Stewardship is God using them to care for that which is His. Prayer is our petitioning God as we seek to do His will. As church ushers, you are God's stewards.

He has entrusted the keeping of the holy temple to you that you may be a watchful eye over the entire service in a way as to give help to the minister by so greeting people that they will be in such a frame of mind, they will receive and accept the Gospel.

✝

As ushers, keeping in mind that you cannot be good stewards of God if you are not consecrated Christians, you must be on the job at all times and carry yourselves in such a way that you will be fit to be called God's faithful stewards.

To be this kind of steward means, neither a tithe of one's wealth, a tenth of one's time, or a part of one's spiritual nature is enough. All of these are included in a life of stewardship, but every part and particle of one's being must be involved in Christian Stewardship.

Your service extends to the Sunday School, Morning Service, Special Programs, Prayer Service, Afternoon, Night, Evangelistic Services, the Lord's Supper, Weddings, Funerals and many other things within the framework of your Christian service.

Now, as ushers, try to fill your place as God's stewards the very best you can in your weak and humble way.

USHERS' MEETINGS
AND A SUGGESTED PROGRAM
TO FOLLOW AT EACH MEETING

Regular meetings of an usher group should be practiced just as any other auxiliary; their date should be well known among themselves as well as to the church proper; their time and place of meeting should be agreed upon and an announcement of this should be made publicly from time to time.

At each of these meetings the regular routine business should be taken up, and the presiding officer will do well to call the roll to know the number present and the number absent each time. The absentees should be accounted for; that is to say, if Brother John Doe or Sister Mary Doe, are both absent when their names are called, someone present should know why they are absent, and if they do not know, an inquiry as to their health, whether they are sick or well, whether they are in or out of the city, should be made and they should be contacted at the earliest possible convenience.

The minutes of the previous meeting should be read, and after a quorum is declared present, then the order of business should be read by the secretary of the group, showing what is to come up for consideration at this particular meeting.

The regular meeting may be held at the church or at the residence of some of the members, this to be agreed upon by a majority of members, but if they take no such action, then the president or chairman of the Board, through the secretary, should call the meeting.

Literary features, such as recitations, solos, reading and addresses from well-known persons could be some of the numbers on the program that would be helpful.

New items touching upon the religious work, taken from some religious publications would not be out of place to bring before meeting for information and inspiration.

The work of other usher groups brought by some member of the church as to how that organization is helping said church would be a fine procedure.

No meeting should be opened without a period of devotion, such as a song, Scripture reading or prayer. A sentence prayer would help a great deal, for it is one of the training departments of the church.

CHURCH COVENANT

Having been led, as we believe, by the Spirit of God to receive the Lord Jesus Christ as our Savior; and on the profession of our faith, having been baptized in the name of the Father, and of the Son, and of the Holy Spirit, we do now in the presence of God, angels and this assembly, most solemnly and joyfully enter into covenant with one another, as one body in Christ.

We engage, therefore, by the aid of the Holy Spirit, to walk together in Christian love; to strive for the advancement of this church in knowledge and holiness; to give it a place in our affection, prayers and service above every organization of human origin; to sustain its worship, ordinances, discipline and doctrines; to contribute cheerfully and regularly, as God has prospered us, towards its expenses, for the support of a faithful and evangelical ministry among us, the relief of the poor and the spread of the Gospel throughout the world. In case of difference of opinion in the church, we will strive to avoid a contentious spirit, and if we cannot unanimously agree, we will cheerfully recognize the right of the majority to govern.

We also engage to maintain family and secret devotion; to study diligently the Word of God; to religiously educate our children; to seek the salvation of our kindred and acquaintance; to walk circumspectly in the world; to be kind and just to those in our employ, and faithful in the service we promise others; endeavoring in the purity of heart and good will towards all men to exemplify and commend our holy faith.

We further engage to watch over, to pray for, to exhort and stir up each other unto every good word and work; to guard each other's reputation, not needlessly exposing the infirmities of others; to participate in each other's joys, and with tender sympathy bear one another's burdens and sorrows; to cultivate Christian courtesy; to be slow to give or take offense, but always ready for recon- ciliation, being mindful of the rules of the Savior in the eighteenth chapter of Matthew, to secure it without delay; and through life, amid evil reports and good reports, to seek to live in the glory of God, who hath called us out of darkness into His marvelous light.

When we move from this place, we engage as soon as possible to unite with some other church where we can carry out the spirit of this covenant and the principles of God's Word.

PARLIAMENTARY LAWS GOVERNING AN USHER BOARD

We suggest, herewith, a simple form of parliamentary usages that may be used as a guide to assist ushers to familiarize themselves as parliamentarians, and to be used in all meetings where questions arise that cannot be set- tled by common consent.

INTRODUCING BUSINESS

No question is properly put before an assembly until a motion placing it before the body is made, seconded and stated by the chair. Prior to such action all debate upon a question is out of order.*

Exceptions: (a) Business is sometimes introduced by the presentation of communications.

(b) Committee reports may be received without formal motions being made to the effect. By receiving a report is meant the simple reading of it.

(c) Three motions that demand no second: (1) Call for the order of the day; (2) a question of order; (3) objections to the consideration of a question.

(d) Sometimes questions are decided by common consent without the formality of a motion.

GRADES OF MOTION

There are four distinct grades of motions made in deliberative assemblies:

(a) Principal or main motions.

(b) Subsidiary or secondary motions.

(c) Incidental questions or motions.

(d) Privileged questions or motions.

MOTIONS EXPLAINED

I. A Principal or main motion is a motion intended to introduced any particular subject to an assembly. A motion of this character can only be made when there is no other question before the house.

---

* Whenever a motion is made involving more than one proposition, a motion is in order to divide the question. If carried, each proposition must be voted on separately.

✝

II. Subsidiary motions are such motions as are made to apply to other motions with a view to disposing of them. Subsidiary motions are as follows:

Lay on the table.
The previous question.
Postpone to a certain day.
Commit, recommit, or refer.
Amend.
Postpone indefinitely.

III. Incidental questions are questions that spring out of the other questions, and are as follows:

Appeal (or questions of order).
Objection to the consideration of a question.
The reading of papers.
Leave to withdraw a motion.
Suspension of the rules.

IV. Privileged questions are questions that by virtue of their great importance take precedence over all other questions and displace all other questions when introduced. They are as follows:

To fix the time of which to adjourn.
Adjourn.
Questions relating to the rights and privileges of the assembly or of any of its members.
Calls for the order of the day.

V. (a) Principal or main motions occupy the lowest grade, as they take precedence over nothing – that is, nothing as to stand aside for such motions.

✿

(b) Subsidiary or secondary motions are superior in point of rank to principal or main motions, as they can be introduced when the former are before the house, and though introduced last, must be disposed of before you can proceed to consider a principal or main motion.

(c) Incidental motions are superior to principal or main motions and to subsidiary or secondary motions.

(d) Privileged questions are the highest grade of motions.

VI. Subsidiary or secondary motions are six in number and have a rank among themselves. Incidental questions have each a rank among themselves. In articles II, III, and IV, under "Motions Explained," each set of motions is there, given according to their rank among themselves.

VII. Taking subsidiary or secondary, incidental, and privileged questions as a whole, their rankings are as follows:

1. To fix the time to which to adjourn (Privileged). Take precedence of all others. In order after the assembly has voted or adjourn, if the vote has not been announced by the chairman. It can be made when another member has the floor, in which case it is undebatable; debatable under other circumstances. Can be amended as to time.

2. To adjourn (Privileged). Superior to all motions, save the one just named above. This is not debatable and cannot be amended. No subsidiary motion may apply to it. It cannot be reconsidered. If lost, it may be repeated after any further business is transacted, if it be but progress in debate.

3. Questions of privilege (Privileged). This is the third motion in point of rank. If important, it is in order while another member has the floor. This is decided by the chairman. Upon an appeal that obtains a second, it is decided by the house. It may be deferred, laid on the table, or be acted upon by any subsidiary motion. When decided, business is resumed at the point where the question was raised.

4. Order of the day (Privileged). This motion is fourth in rank, but does not take precedence over the motion to reconsider. It is not debatable and requires no second. This is in order when another member has the floor.

5. Appeal (Incidental). This motion requires a second and cannot be amended. It is undebatable when the question is one of indecorum, or transgressions of the rules of debate, as to priority of business, or if made when the previous question is before the house. It can be laid on the table, and previous question may be applied to it, without in either case effecting anything save the appeal. A vote on an appeal may be reconsidered.

6. Objections to the consideration of a question (Incidental). Objections can be made to the consideration of principal motions, if made when the subject is first introduced. They can be made while another member has the floor. Does not need a second. They cannot be debated, amended, or affected by any other subsidiary motion.

7. Reading papers (Incidental). Any member may call for the reading of papers before the assembly for consid-

eration, and he has a right to expect his request to be granted. If objected to, a motion is made granting the desired privilege. This motion cannot be debated or amended.

8. Withdrawal of a motion (Incidental). A motion may be withdrawn by the mover, if no one objects; if objected to, a motion granting permission to withdraw must be made. Such a motion cannot be debated or amended.

9. Suspension of the rules (Incidental). Is not debatable. Cannot be amended. No other subsidiary motion may be applied to it. A vote on suspension cannot be reconsidered. Must be for a definite purpose. This requires a two-third vote.

10. Lay on the table (Subsidiary). Is preeminent over all debatable questions, but is subordinate to privileged and incidental questions and to lay on the table. Gives way to a motion to adjourn. Cannot prevent a motion being made to lay main subject on the table, even after the previous question is ordered. It is not debatable and cannot be amended. Applies to questions of privilege as well as to all other debatable questions.

"If adopted, its effect is as follows:

(1) Its effect (expecting when to Amend or to Commit is pending) is to instantly close debate, and bring the assembly to a vote upon the pending question. The vote being taken, the effect of the previous question is exhausted, and the business before the assembly stands exactly as if the vote on the pending motion had been taken in the

usual way, without having been forced to it by the previous question; so if this vote is reconsidered the question is divested of the previous question, and is again open to debate.

(2) Its effect when either of the motions to Amend or to Commit is pending, is to cut off debate, and to force a vote, not only upon the motions to amend and to commit, but also upon the question to be amended or committed. The chairman puts to vote all these questions in their order of precedence, beginning with the one last move (see illustrations further on). The previous questions, or else it has been voted to refer the subject to a committee. If one of these votes is reconsidered before the previous question is exhausted, the tendency of the previous question precludes debate upon the motion reconsidered.

The motion for the previous question may be limited to the pending amendment, and if adopted, debate is closed on the amendment only. After the amendment is voted on, the main question is again open to debate and amendment. (In case the form of the question would be similar to this, "Shall the question be put now on amendment?") So in the same manner it can be moved on an amendment of an amendment.

The object of the previous question is to bring the assembly to a vote on the question put before it without further debate.

An appeal from the decision of the chair is undebatable if made after the previous question has been moved, and before final action has been taken under it.

To illustrate the effect of the previous question under all kinds of circumstances, take the following examples:

(a) Suppose a question is before the assembly, and an amendment to it is offered, and then it is moved to postpone the question to another time: the previous question now being ordered stops the debate and forces a vote on the pending question–the postponement. When that vote is taken, the effect of the previous is exhausted. If the assembly refuses to postpone the subject, the debate is resumed upon the pending amendment.

(b) Suppose the subject under consideration is interrupted by a question of privilege, and it has been moved to refer this latter question to a committee: the previous question being now ordered brings the assembly to a vote first on the motion to commit, and if that motion fails, next on the privilege question. After the privileged question is voted on, the previous question is exhausted and the consideration of the subject which was interrupted is resumed.

(c) Suppose, again, that while an amendment to the question is pending a motion is made to refer the subject to a committee, and some one moves to amend this last motion by giving the committee instructions; in addition to the main question we have here only the motion to amend and to commit, and therefore the previous question, if ordered, applies to them all as one question. The chairman immediately puts the question (1) on the committee's instruction, (2) on the motion to commit, and if this be adopted the subject is exhausted; but if it fails, next (3) on the amendment, and finally (4) on the main question.

11. To postpone to a certain day (Subsidiary). This motion takes precedence of motion to commit, or amend, or indefinitely postpone. It steps aside for any privileged or incidental question, to lay on the table, or for the question. It can be amended as to time. It allows for limited debate, and is confined to the propriety of adopting the date specified. If adopted, the subject is disposed or cannot be taken up before the house designated, save by a two thirds vote.

12. To amend (Subsidiary). This motion takes precedence of nothing but the question to which it is applied, and yields to all privileged, incidental, or subsidiary questions, except to indefinitely postpone. A motion to amend must bear directly upon and be germane to, the motion desire amended, though it may be directly the reverse in sentiment to that motion. It can be amended by adding or inserting, striking out some and inserting others.

No amendment is allowable to any of the following motions:

To adjourn.
For the order of the day.
All incidental questions.
To lay on the table.

For the previous question.

An amendment of an amendment.

To postpone indefinitely.

To record.

13.   To postpone indefinitely (Subsidiary). It cannot be applied to any save a principal motion. It yields to all privileged, incidental, and subsidiary motions, except to amend. It opens the entire question to debate. It cannot be amended. The previous question being ordered on it does not affect the main question.

THE MOTION TO RECONSIDER, ETC.

When any principal or main motion (or amendment) has once been acted upon by an assembly, it cannot be had under consideration again at the same meeting without a motion to reconsider it having been introduced and adopted. This motion must be made by a person who voted with the majority or the original question, must be made on the same day, and, if lost, it (the motion to reconsider) cannot be renewed on that question.

A motion to rescind may be made by any member when he desires to have the assembly annual some previous action. This motion is made when a motion to reconsider would be too late. Any action of an assembly may be annulled by the passing of this motion, regardless of the time that has elapsed since the taking of such action.

A correction in the minutes may be made at any time without the necessity of a motion to reconsider.

A motion to adjourn, if lost, can be renewed without a motion to reconsider, provided any business has been transacted since it was originally made, even if such business is but progress in debate.

A motion to reconsider is in order even when another member has the floor, but it cannot be considered while another question is before the body.

On the subject of the motion to reconsider, Roberts' "Rules of Order" speak quite well, as follows:

"A motion to reconsider the vote on a Subsidiary Motion takes precedence of the main question. It yields to Privileged questions (except for the Order of the Day) and Incidental Questions."

"This motion can be applied to the vote on every other question, except to adjourn and to suspend the rules, and an affirmative vote on, to Lay on the Table or to Take from the Table, and a vote electing to office one who is present and does not decline. No question can be twice reconsidered, unless it was amended after its first reconsideration. If an amendment to a motion has been either adopted or rejected, and then a vote taken on the motion as amended, it is not in order to reconsider the vote on the amendment until after the vote on the original motion has been reconsidered. If the previous question has been partly executed, it cannot be reconsidered. This motion cannot be amended; it is debatable or undebatable. When debatable, it opens up for discussion the entire subject to be reconsidered, and the previous question, if ordered while it is pending, affects only the motion to reconsider. It can be laid on the table, in which case, the reconsideration, like any other question, can be taken from the table, but possesses no privilege. The motion to reconsider being laid on the table does not carry with it the pending measure.

"The effect of making this motion is to suspend all action that the original motion would have required until the reconsideration is acted upon; but if it is not called up, its effect terminates with the session provided, that in an assembly having regular meetings as often as monthly, if there is no help upon another day an adjourned meeting of the one at which the reconsideration of an Incidental or Subsidiary Motion (except where the vote to be reconsidered had the effect to receive the whole subject from before the assembly) shall be immediately acted upon, as otherwise it would prevent action on the main question."

"While this motion is so highly privileged as far as it relates to having it entered on the minutes, yet the reconsideration of another question cannot be made to interfere with the discussion of a question before the assembly, but as soon as that subject is disposed of, the reconsideration, if called up, takes precedence of everything except the motion to adjourn, and to fix the time at which to adjourn. As long as its effects last (as shown above) anyone can call up the motion to reconsider, and have it acted upon – except when its effect extends beyond the meeting at which the motion was made no one but the mover can bring it up at that meeting."

"This effect of the adoption of this motion is to place before the assembly the original question in the exact position it occupied before it was voted upon; consequently, no one can debate the question reconsidered who had previously exhausted his right to debate on that question; his only resource is before the assembly. When a vote taken under the operation of the previous question is reconsidered, the question is then divested of the previous question is reconsidered, the question is then divested of the previous question and is open to debate and amendment, provided the previous question has been exhausted by vote taken on all the questions covered by it, before the motion to reconsider was made."

"A reconsideration requires only a majority vote, regardless of the vote necessary to adopt the motion reconsidered."

MOTIONS
REQUIRING A TWO-THIRDS VOTE

The following motions require a two-thirds vote in order to be adopted:

To amend the rules.

To suspend the rules.

To make a special order.

To take up a question out of its proper order.

An objection to the consideration of a question.

To extend the limits of debate.

To close or limit debate.

The previous question.

Expulsion of members.

A motion to amend can be amended, but an amendment to an amendment cannot be amended.

UNDEBATABLE MOTIONS

The following motions are undebatable:

To adjourn.

Appeal relating to decorum.

☦

Call to order.
Motion of close debate.
Motion to extend limits of debate.
Leave to continue speaking after indecorum.
To lay on the table.
Motion to limit debate.
Object to the consideration of a question.
Motion for the order of the day.
Previous question.
Questions relating to priority of business.
Reading papers.
Reconsider an undebatable question.
Suspend the rules.
Take from the table.
Take up a question out of its proper order.
Withdrawal of a motion.

OBTAINING RECOGNITION

Before a member can make a motion or speak upon a question, he must first obtain recognition from the chairperson.

The following consideration should govern a chairperson in granting the floor:

(a) The member first obtaining the floor.

(b) When two or more obtain the floor at the same time, the one farthest away gets to speak first.

(c) When issues are clearly drawn on a subject, and there are two parties, recognition should be given first to one side of the controversy, and then to the other.

(d) The chairperson of a committee making a report is usually accorded the floor if he has not previously spoken, even if others succeed in getting to their feet before he does. It is his right also to close debate.

(e) If the chair is in doubt as to who obtained the floor first, or as to who should have recognition, he may submit it to the house to decide by vote.

(f) If a member feels himself entitled to the floor after the chairperson has decided against him, he may make an appeal from the decision of the chair.

(g) No member who has spoken once on the subject is entitled to the floor a second time until every other member so desiring has spoken, except by unanimous consent.

SPECIAL MEETINGS

Sometimes emergencies arise that render necessary or expedient a special meeting of parties interested in a given subject. A meeting is called and the parties solicited to be present should come.

Anyone familiar with the object of the meeting may, at the hour designated for opening, call the body together, briefly state the purpose of the meeting, and invite nominations for temporary chairperson.

When a vote is taken and a temporary chairperson is elected, the person calling this meeting to order surrenders the meeting to the chairperson. A temporary secretary is next chosen.

A committee is then appointed to bring in nominations for permanent officers. When this has been done and the permanent officers have been elected, the gathering is in a condition to proceed with the matter for which it was called together.

It is usually the case that a committee is appointed to retire and bring in resolutions bearing on the subject in order to get it into tangible form for action. If it is a matter that demands extended consideration, the meeting ordinarily adjourns subject to the call of the chairperson; the chairperson keeps in touch with the committee appointed, and when informed that they are ready to report, issues the call.

If the matter is of such a nature that one meeting will suffice, while the committee is out deliberating, speeches are usually heard from prominent person known to be in sympathy with the movement.

If it is the object of the meeting to form a permanent organization, the task of the committee is to draw up a suitable constitution and by-laws. When this is done and the report is adopted, it is proper to proceed to organize under the constitution.

COMMITTEE REPORTS

When a committee has been assigned a task to perform, and has finished or is ready to report, the chairperson of the committee gains the attention of the chairperson of the usher's group and states that he is ready to report.

A motion to receive the report is sometimes made but more often it is received – that is, heard – it is in order to move, to accept, to adopt, or reject, or recommit.

If the committee has findings, they may be accepted or rejected; if it makes recommendations, they may be adopted or not or if the report does not suite the entire

✝

group (majority), it may be recommitted or sent back to the committee.

The body may also instruct the committee as to what to include in a report.

VOTING

"Whenever from the nature of the question it permits no modification or debate, the chairperson immediately puts it to a vote; if the question is debatable, when the chairperson thinks the debate has been brought to a close, he should inquire if the assembly is ready for the question, and if no one rises he puts the question to vote."

There are various forms of putting the question in use in different parts of the country.

The rule in Congress, in the House of Representatives, requires questions to be put in as follows:

"As many as are in favor (as the question may be) say Aye"; and after the affirmative voice is expressed, "As many as are opposed say No."

The following forms are very common: "It has been moved and second that (here state the question) as many as are in favor of the motion say Aye; those opposed, No."

Or if the motion is for the adoption of a certain resolution, after it has been read the chairperson can say, "You have heard the resolution read; those in favor of its adoption will hold up the right hand; those opposed will manifest it by the same sign."

These examples are sufficient to show the usual methods of putting a question, the affirmative being always put first.

"A majority vote, that is, a majority of the votes cast ignoring blanks, is sufficient for the adoption of any motion that is in order, except those which require a two-thirds vote. A plurality vote never adopts a motion nor elects any one except by virtue of a special rule previously adopted."

When a vote is taken, the chairperson should always announce the result in the following form: "The motion is carried – the resolution is adopted," or "The ayes have it – the resolution is adopted."

If, when he announces a vote, any member rises and states that he doubts the vote, or calls for a "division," the chairperson shall say, "A division is called for; those in favor of the motion will rise." After counting these, and announcing the number, he shall say, "Those opposed will rise."

He will count these, announce the number, and declare the result; that is, whether the motion is carried or lost. Instead of counting the vote himself, he can direct the secretary, or appoint tellers, to make the count and report to him. When tellers are appointed, they should be selected from both sides of the question.

A member has the right to change his vote (when not made by ballot) before the decision of the question has been finally and conclusively pronounced by the chairperson, but not afterwards.

Until the negative is put, it is in order for any member, in the same manner as if the voting had not been commenced, to rise and speak, make motions for amendment or otherwise, and thus renew the debate; and this, whether the member was in an assembly or not when the question was put the vote partly taken.

After the chairperson has announced the vote, if it is found that a member has risen and addressed the chair before the negative had been put, he is entitled to be heard on the question, the same as though the vote had not been taken. In such cases, the question is in the same condition as if it had never been put.

No one can vote on a question affecting himself; but if more than one name is included in the resolution (though a sense of delicacy would prevent this right being exercised, except when it would change the vote) all are entitled to vote; for if this were not so, a majority could control an assembly by including the names of a sufficient number in a motion, say for preferring charges against them, and suspend them, or even expel them from the assembly.

When there is a tie vote the motion fails, unless the chairperson gives his vote for the affirmative, which he is at liberty to do, as he has a right to vote whenever his vote will affect the result. When his vote in the negative will make a tie, he can cast it and thus defeat the measure. In case of an Appeal, though the question is, "Shall the decision of the chair stand as the judgment of the assembly?" A tie vote sustains the chair, upon the principle that the decision of the chair can only be reserved by a majority.

Another form of voting is by ballot. This method is adopted only when required by the constitution or by-laws of the assembly, or when the assembly has ordered the vote to be so taken. The chairperson, in such cases, appoints at least two tellers, who distribute slips of paper, upon which each member, including the chairperson, writes his vote. In voting by ballot, members are not restricted to persons who have been nominated.

Closing nominations prevent the public endorsement of any other candidates, but does not prevent their being voted for and being elected.

When the votes are collected, they are counted by the tellers, and the result reported to the chairperson who announces it to the assembly.

The chairperson announces the result of the vote, in case of an election to office, in a manner similar to the following: the whole number of votes cast is _____; the number necessary for an election is _____. Mr. A. received _____; Mr. B. _____; Mr. C. _____: Mr. B. having received the required number, is elected _____.

Where there is only one candidate for an office, and the constitution requires the vote to be by ballot, it is common to authorize the clerk to cast the vote of the assembly for such and such a person; if anyone objects, however, it is necessary to ballot in the usual way.

So, when a motion is made to make a vote unanimous, it fails if anyone objects. In counting the ballots all blanks are ignored. The assembly can, by a majority vote, order that the vote on any question be taken by Yeas and Nays.

In this method of voting, the chairperson states both sides of the question at once; the clerk calls the roll, and each member, as his name is called, rises and answers Yes or No, and the clerk notes his answer.

✟

Upon the completion of the roll call, the clerk reads over the names of those who answered in the affirmative, and afterwards, those in the negative, that mistakes may be corrected; he then gives the number voting on each side to the chairperson, who announces the result.

An entry must be made in the minutes of the names of all voting in the affirmative, and also of those in the negative.

"The form of putting a question upon which the vote has been ordered to be taken by yeas and nays is similar to the following:

"As many as are in favor of the adoption of these resolutions will, when their names are called, answer Yes (or Aye); those opposed will answer No."

The chairperson will then direct the clerk to call the roll. The negative being put at the same time as the affirmative, it is too late, after one person has answered to the roll call, to renew the debate. After the commencement of the roll call it is too late to ask to be excused from voting.

A WORD TO PRESIDING OFFICERS

Upon the presiding officer, more than upon any one else, depends the successful transaction of business.

It behooves a presiding officer to be thoroughly posted in general parliamentary law.

He should bear in mind that it is the purpose of the rules to aid, not to hinder, bodies in the transaction of business.

He should bear this in mind in all his rulings.

If at any time a chairperson discovers himself to be in error, or if an error is pointed out to him, he will do well to at once admit his mistake. To persist in it will only serve to make matters worse.

The chairperson can do much to help along proceedings by pointing out to the members the proper kinds of motions to make to reach the ends sought by them.

He should be able to rule readily upon any situation, however complicated, and thus save the body from hopeless tangles.

The chairperson should maintain an impartial attitude on all questions under consideration before a body, ruling according to law regardless of his personal desire as to the outcome of the deliberations.

When desirous of taking part in a debate, the chairpersons should vacate the chair for the time being and call the vice-chairperson or some other person to occupy it. He should rarely take such a course, as participation is partisan debate, for this tends to impair his influence as a presiding officer.

He should keep a parliamentary guide by his side when presiding.

Above all, he should always be calm and collected, never losing self-control. A chairperson that cannot control himself, cannot hope to guide others to self-control.

SUGGESTED SIGNAL CODE*

Question – What is the signal from the front usher to the usher in the back of the aisle, letting them know you wish to seat them?

Answer – Extend your hand politely, keeping the elbow close to the body.

Question – What is the signal from the usher in the aisle to the usher in charge to send a relief at once?

Answer – Face the door and put one finger of the right hand straight across the chest.

Question – What is the signal from the usher in the aisle to the usher in charge requiring church literature or program?

Answer – Point the first two (2) fingers of the right hand straight across the breast.

Question – What is the signal from the usher in the aisle to the usher in charge to send contribution envelopes at once?

Answer – Point three (3) fingers of the right hand straight across the breast.

Question – What is the signal from the usher in the aisle to the usher in charge to send someone for a message?

Answer – Hold the first fingers of the right hand about face high until you have the attention of the usher in charge.

---

* Every time you give a signal to the usher in charge, face the door where the usher in charge is.

✟

Question – What is the signal from the usher in the aisle to the usher in charge informing him that seats are available in his or her aisle or section?

Answer – Right hand up about face high, palm out if more than three (3) seats; otherwise designate number of seats by number of fingers. If no seats are available, right hand up with fingers closed.

NOTES

✝

NOTES

✞